369 MANIFESTING JOURNAL

THE KEY TO YOUR DREAM LIFE. LAW OF
ATTRACTION AND MANIFESTATION CRASH
COURSE WITH GUIDED 369 BOOK

ELIZABETH PARKER

INTRODUCTION

Manifestation Method 369 is a set of actions based on the principles of the **Law of Attraction.** Manifestation directs you towards your goals by helping you focus on your intentions.

In order to attract the results you desire, you must be persistent in your practice so that you achieve the desired level of motivation.

In other words, you have to align your mind, your actions to wards your goals.

The theory behind it is that thoughts in the forefront of your mind are more likely to be detected and grasped.

If an idea does not remain at the forefront of your mind, you are more likely to go on autopilot throughout the day. You will lose the opportunities that come towards you and it will take longer to achieve your goals.

Manifestation Method 369 requires not only mental manifestation but also active actions; it is not possible to attract a new relationship without actively seeking to meet new people.

The 'Method of Manifestation 369' was discovered by Nikola Tesla and at the basis of this Method there are three numbers: 3, 6 and 9. These numbers are also called divine numbers and, according to the Serbian scientist, they contain in themselves the key to the universe.

If you want to discover the secrets of the universe, think in terms of energy, frequency and vibration.

- Nikola Tesla

Everything in the universe is energy, you can also see this with a concrete example from everyday life. What unit of measurement is energy? The Joule indicated by the letter J.

You may have noticed that two items are indicated on food labels: Kcal and KJ. When you eat, what you are doing is introducing energy into your body.

You are energy, your thoughts are energy and they can be used as a magnet to attract what you desire into your life.

Manifestation Method 369 is based on the premise that similar energies are attracted by each other. This means that positive energy will attract other positive energy, conversely, negative energy will attract other negative energy.

Whether you are an optimist or a pessimist, you can benefit from the incredible power of Method 369.

The former will probably be facilitated to attract positive thoughts, the latter will have to train a bit more as he needs to improve his outlook on things. However, success stories teach us that it is not your starting point that is important but how motivated and hungry you are towards your goals.

Leonardo Del Vecchio, founder of Luxottica started from the bottom and in the course of his life he managed to create the multinational that dominates the eyewear sector.

It is proven that with Manifestation Method 369 the time required to attract something to you is greatly reduced.

As we will see later, the number 3 connects directly to the universe, 6 represents inner strength and the number 9 helps you to let all the negative energies go.

The purpose of this book is to give you an overview of the method so that you can get to know the theoretical basis of this system. In addition to the theory, I also want to associate a practical part, contained in **Chapter 9, so** that you can experience first- hand what I will tell you about in the rest of this book.

If you are reading this manuscript right now, it is because consciously or unconsciously you have wanted to attract it to you, you want to improve your life and this book is the one for you.

Accept this gift from the universe with gratitude, and you will have all the tools you need to achieve the success you desire and deserve.

1

THE INVENTOR WHO REVOLUTIONISED THE PHYSICAL AND METAPHYSICAL WORLD

The man credited with the discovery of the 369 Manifestation Method is Nikola Tesla, who is considered one of the most brilliant minds of the 20th century.

Tesla was born in a Serbian family in what is now Croatia on 10th July 1856. Since his birth, Tesla has had a very interesting story. In fact, his mother said that little NiKola was born during a thunderstorm.

These natural events were once considered a bad omen, even if the woman was convinced that the child was 'the child of light'.

Tesla later moved to the United States where he met and collaborated at the beginning with Thomas Edison and then with George Westinghouse. It was at this stage of his life that the scientist discovered that the earth's standing waves could resonate at a certain electrical frequency'.

This scientific discovery was what enabled him to light 200 wireless lamps from 25 miles away, even producing flashes from 135 feet.

Tesla had a soft spot for the mysteries of the world and in his autobiography, he reveals us out-of-body sensations from him childhood. He also tells us of seeing places with the same sharpness and 'intensity' as he saw them in everyday life.

Perhaps this connection was behind Tesla's ability to make frighteningly accurate predictions and sharpen his acute senses.

In 1926, Tesla said that the whole world would be 'converted into a huge brain... we will see and hear each other as perfectly as if we were face to face... compared to our present telephone. A man will be able to carry it in his vest pocket' (Milojkovic, 2020).

So did Tesla foresee the use of modern technology, such as smartphones and video calls?

The scientist also believed in renewable energy sources and had encouraged his contemporary colleagues to find a way to use solar and wind power to produce electricity 120 years before the renewable energy activism began.

Tesla is not the only one who has told similar stories, great sport champions such as Michael Jordan has also revealed that he has had mystical visions. We will delve into the visualisation techniques necessary to increase and accelerate the effectiveness of the manifestations of Method 369 later in this book.

"If you knew the magnificence of 3, 6 and 9, you would have a key to the universe" - Nikola Tesla

2

THE NUMBERS 3, 6, 9 IN THE WORLD

Starting with the words of the famous engineer '*If you knew the magnificence of 3, 6 and 9, you would have a key to the universe*', we can see the presence of the numbers 3, 6, 9 also in history, ancient religion, modern science, anatomy and many other fields.

Numbers 3, 6, and 9 have a special significance in modern science and are used simply as a means to describe the physical properties of the universe. In nature, we find it in the subatomic particles that create atoms (protons, neutrons and electrons). If we consider the aspect of faith, number 3 often recurs in different religion as we will instance in a moment.

In the Egyptian religion, the presence of numbers 3,6,9, is clearly visible, in fact you can find the god of heaven, the god of earth and the god of the abyss.

This trinity also appears in Greek mythology with Zeus, Poseidon and Hades, who rule the sky, the earth, the sea and the underworld respectively. This triplicity can also be found in the

Christian Holy Trinity with: the Father, the Son and the Holy Spirit.

In Buddhism, number 3 represents the Three Jewels (Buddha, Dhamma, Sangha), which are considered the pillars of Buddhism.

In Hinduism, number 6 represents the cyclical nature of life and death.

In Jewish Kabbalah, number 9 represents wisdom and enlightenment; in Islam, number 9 represents completeness and unity. The Prophet Muhammad said that God is One and the prayer consists of 9 parts.

If we look at our body, we can see that it consists of three main organs: the heart, the lungs and the brain.

The absence of one or more of these three fundamental organs, our organism ceases to function.

The pineal gland, also known as the "third eye", is worth mentioning. According to many scholars, this gland in our brain has the function of giving man the sixth sense.

These are some examples of how numbers 3, 6, 9 are present in the world and in the organisms that populate it.

3

THE MATHEMATICAL MAGIC OF NUMBERS 3, 6, 9

Mathematics was not created by man, it was only discovered by man. This science is a universal law and no matter who you are or where you live, two plus two will always be four.

According to scientist Marko Rodin, numbers 3, 6 and 9 represent a 'flow field' or vector of the third and fourth dimensions' (2021).

The basic idea is that when you double each number, starting with one, you will never get 3, 6 and 9; instead you will get a repeated sequence of numbers 1, 2, 4, 8, 7 and 5.

The scientist believes that this flow field is a source of higher energy from another dimension.

Someone suggests that this can be a source of free energy, while others believe that using these numbers can open a door to revitalising personal energy.

Tesla was known to be particularly obsessive about numbers, but he had a predilection for numbers 3, 6 and 9, claiming that they had greater significance than any other number series.

To understand why Tesla considered these numbers so important, we must delve into understanding their numerological significance.

Nothing exists in the universe except mathematical fixity points. - Albert Einstein

4

THE HIDDEN MEANING OF NUMBERS 3, 6, 9

In numerology, 3 represents creativity and artistic expression. It also indicates growth and development, both personal and professional.

Number 3 is related to communication, socialising, relationships and it is also a symbol of optimism and joy. It is considered a number of luck and success, especially for those with a strong artistic and creative aptitude.

It is the number of expansion and growth, encouraging you to explore new opportunities and express yourself more authentically.

This number also represents balance and harmony. It describes the ability to find a balance between work and personal life. It encourages you to develop healthy and long lasting relationships and to communicate effectively with others.

It represents beauty, joy, creativity and urges you to follow your dreams and express your true nature.

Number 6 represents love, care and responsibility. It symbolises balance, harmony, the importance of helping others and creating a safe and secure environment.

Number 6 is associated with family, home, community, it represents the idea of 'home' in both the literal and metaphorical sense.

It also indicates the ability to solve problems and find creative solutions. It encourages you to take care of yourself and others in a balanced and harmonious way.

Number 6 is also associated with faith, spirituality as it represents the ability to follow your values and trust yourself and others.

It stimulates you to create lasting and meaningful relationships and to build a life full of love and support.

Number 9 embodies the completion and the end of a cycle, symbolising the end of one phase of life and the beginning of a new one. It is considered the number of conclusion and resolution, encouraging you to let past go.

It represents the ability to see the picture as a whole and to have a global perspective, prompting one to observe the world with an open mind and a heart full of compassion.

Number 9 is also associated with generosity, philanthropy and leadership, it represents the ability to serve others and make the difference in the world.

It pushes you to be an example for others, to live authentically and consistently with your values.

When all these three numbers are together, they create a structure that opens the door t o expansion and growth.

5

THE FOUNDATIONS OF METHOD 369
AND THE LAW OF ATTRACTION

The law of attraction was made famous by the book 'The Secret' published by Rhonda Byrne. This manuscript contains several examples of the Law of Attraction and the manifestation of desires

This philosophy asserts that people can emanate positive thoughts and energy into the universe and receive more positive energy in return.

This process works with both positive and negative thoughts. That is precisely why at the beginning of this book, I wrote that this manuscript is suitable for all people, both optimists and pessimists.

Amplified and a abundant energy can return to you if you chose to give positive energy to the world.

As we have seen before, everything is energy, even your thoughts.

If you want to discover the secrets of the universe, think in terms of energy, frequency and vibration.

- Nikola Tesla

Method 369 uses this concept to attract anything you want into your life, from health to money even to relationships.

The law of attraction has very ancient roots comparable to the principles of karma or the biblical verse 'Do not do to others what you would not want others to do to you.

Even though there is still no scientific basis proving the validity of the law of attraction, a 2005 study found out that people with positive affection were more likely to enjoy high levels of happiness and success.

I ask you this question: has negativity ever given you anything but more negativity?

Every time you complain because bad things are always happening to you or you focus on all the things you don't have or would like to have without a single positive thought, you are engaging in the law of attraction, only you are doing so towards negative energies.

A research from Stanford University has shown that complaining reduces the size of your hippocampus, the region of the brain which is crucial for problem solving.

Furthermore, this study pointed out that constantly complaining makes it easier to complain in the future, and this will have a negative impact on your ability to think positively and focus on the good.

Therefore, the negativity resulting from complaints will attract more negativity and start a horrible cycle.

Break the spiral of complaints and focus on good and positive things, will lead you to manifest the results you want and the success you desire.

You have to be aware that the best way to manifest using the law of attraction is the present moment.

The past is past, the future has not arrived yet, so however imperfect your present may seem, it is the only element you can act on to improve your life.

Each present moment can be improved over and over again until it becomes what you wish to attract.

Last but not least, remember to express gratitude in every instant, this will allow you to see with new eyes and have a new perspective.

You can express gratitude for anything, you can be grateful because 'the anxiety is gone' or 'because the pain in your back has gone away'.

If everything goes wrong, look in the mirror and be thankful because 'Today you are breathing, so you can be thankful for life'.

If you want to improve your life, start focusing on the present moment and attract positive thoughts.

I have not failed. I just found 10,000 ways that won't work. - Thomas A. Edison

6

THE LAW OF ATTRACTION DISCOVERED BY THE ANCIENT ROMANS

After having reached this point, it should be clear to you that like attracts like, whether thoughts, words, people or actions.

In ancient Rome, they used to say 'similibus enim similia gaudent' which literally means: 'Every like loves its like'.

People in fact prefer to spend time with those who have the same interests, merits, faults and tastes. They attract those who reflect themselves, their values and their morals.

You may have noticed this evidence in everyday life. During a date with a man or woman you may realize that you are more attracted to those who have similar values, you may be more interested in people who like the same artist or the same type of film.

Similarities can be found in the world of work, you may be more attracted to colleagues who share the same work ethic as yours, who are willing to take on a similar workload as you are or who know how to complete projects as quickly and efficiently as you do.

These examples are just further proof of the law of attraction. Everything is energy, from your brain to the electronic devices you use every day, everything on this planet has its own energy, its own magnetic field, its own vibration and therefore you can attract it using similar energies, frequencies and vibrations.

7

THE METHOD 369

The most important thing you need to know before you start manifesting is what you want to attract. To help you define what you want to attract, you can ask yourself the following questions:

- What are my needs?
- What are my wishes?
- Do my needs and desires coincide?

There is absolutely no shame in wanting to manifest wealth, a relationship or whatever else your heart desires. When you have discovered what you are looking for, you will formulate affirmations that will help you keep your goal in mind and communicate it to the universe.

By doing so, you will have an affirmation to write, which will increase the effectiveness of the Method.

It is important that you consider what you want to manifest as already realised. For example, you can write 'I am so happy to have been chosen for the role of marketing manager of my company' instead of 'I want to become the marketing manager of my company this year'.

While you are practising writing down your goal you can also imagine yourself having already realised what you wish to manifest. In our example, you can imagine yourself being the

marketing manager of your company and running a successful marketing campaign.

Psychology tells us that imagining what you want to manifest helps you to feel the emotions of success, they are an accelerator in consolidating motivation.

This is due to the fact that the subconscious mind about 90 per cent of the total actions we perform on a daily basis.

A 2010 study showed that visualising your desires increases their likelihood becoming reality. Visualisation techniques have also been used for many years by professional athletes to excel during their performances.

Many are familiar with the famous story of Michael Jordan's poisoned pizza and his mystical visions of that night.

In 1997 the Chicago Bulls were in Utah to play in the NBA finals. The night before the game Jordan was hungry and had some pizzas delivered to his room.

Several hours after that meal the athlete called the medical staff, he was sick, he had been vomiting all night.

The next day Jordan showed up at the arena for the match. In the pre-match Michael stood motionless on the bench and had a towel on his head, everyone thought he was very sick and could not play.

They were wrong, Jordan played, scored 38 points and Chicago won the game, but the story was not over yet.

A few days later Game 6 was played, the two teams were neck-and-neck when the end of the match was near.

Time out.

The Chicago Bulls star knew that in the next play Utah would have defended differently than usual, so Michael called Steve Kerr and explained him how they would have won the game.

The match resumed, Utah changed defence and moved as Jordan had predicted, Kerr scored two points and Chicago won the title.

Some time later Jordan would recount that while he was sick that night he had watched the entire game, imagining every single possession and movement that he would make and that others would make.

The day after being sick while sitting on the bench with the towel resting on his head, Jordan was reviewing what he had seen that night.

This is just one of many stories of athletes who, thanks to visualisation, have succeeded in achieving their goals.

Using this technique together with Manifestation Method 369 you can act to speed up the time it takes to attract your manifestation.

Simplifying, we can say that the 369 Manifestation Method concern in the belief of the achievement of your manifestation. It's about being so sure that success has already arrived such that it aligns the subconscious mind and prompts it to think that you have already achieved a certain goal.

This action breaks the chain of limiting beliefs from the past and helps your brain to function at a higher level so that you finally get closer to your goals.

The Method consists of writing your event, imagining your future and implementing daily steps to help you remember and achieve your goals.

More and more people have claimed that thanks to this Method they have been able to attract wealth, love, their dream job and much more.

Using the meanings of numbers 3, 6 and 9, you are able to connect to a deep source of energy in the universe, recognise your inner strength and expel what no longer serves you.

8

THE METHOD 369 PRACTICAL LESSON

Having reached this point, let us see how and when to manifest during the day.

Your first manifestation should be in the morning, preferably just after waking up. When you open your eyes you manifest by writing in your manifestation diary what you want to attract **three times**.

Having the Manifestation notebook or diary with you at all times is a great way to help you in this process.

When you write your manifestations in the morning, you connect with the universe, with the idea of starting again, and this is represented by the new day. Some people may see this as a connection between themselves and their higher self, because three beings are in the running during this ritual: yourself, the universe and your higher self.

Writing down your manifestation three times promotes creative well-being. It makes you more aware of yourself and what you can do to clear the way from obstacles, so that the universe can give you manifestations with greater abundance.

In the afternoon, write your affirmations **six times**, preferably around three o'clock. This time represents the connection between you and the universe.

Finally, in the evening, write your affirmations **nine times**. You can choose to write your affirmations before going to bed or at nine o'clock, as this time represents the elimination of things you no longer need.

To accelerate and improve the manifestation process, every day, just before falling asleep imagine your goal and state what you want to manifest.

After doing this, imagine the reality you desire for yourself and utter the following statement with firm conviction: '**I trust the universe**'.

I repeat another time with the 369 Manifestation Method you are able to realise all your desires.

But remember manifestation is nothing without action!

Too often people believe that manifestation is akin to blind faith; in reality, it will offer you nothing without proper action.

Manifestation is not something that the universe gives you effortlessly, this means that certain obstacles are necessary and must be overcomed in order to get what you are asking for in your manifestations.

You can see these obstacles as the universe's way of verifying that you are truly determined towards the goal.

After passing these tests, the universe will reward you with what you have asked for it.

Many people have said that demonstrating using pen and paper produces better results than using a digital tool.

This is because you are using your energy to create something in the world. The act of writing words on a piece of paper is creation, and this can be a key element in bringing your dreams into reality.

That is why I advised you at the beginning of this chapter to always have your event diary with you.

Remember to always be grateful too. You should manifest gratitude from the very beginning, even before you have received what you are manifesting; gratitude is a fundamental part of the Method.

You are asking yourself: "Why should I give thanks for something I have not received yet?!"

The answer is very simple, think in these terms:

If you ask someone for something you cannot get, you ask them politely by saying, 'please'.

If someone does you a favor like handing you an object you say 'thank you' as you take it from hands.

Do you remember what is other I told you earlier that it is important to write down your manifestations in the present tense? Here, you have already received from the Universe that is why you must act as if you have just received what you have asked for with your Manifestation.

In this sense 'please' is the magic word and 'thank you' is the formula which let you expres gratitude for having received your manifestation.

How long will you have to wait before you see the first results?

The answer to this question depends on how well you are practising the method and the size of your event.

For example, if in your manifestation, you want to become a professional athlete and participate to the world championships, you will need more time and practice.

In general, there is no fixed time frame, the only key is persistence with energy.

Gabby Bernstein, New York Times bestselling author, states that 'patience is everything' and also adds that if we positively align ourselves with our goals, technically it won't take long to achieve them.

Do your best to avoid obsessing about the arrival date of your event. Even if this is difficult, it is better to stop worrying too much before all your thoughts become consumed. If you have difficulty controlling obsessive thoughts, try distracting yourself with other things, or try with meditation.

The universe works on its own timetable, sometimes the only thing you can do is to make sure the path is clear for your manifestation to become a reality. This means removing anything toxic or negative from your life so that your energy pathways are ready and willing to accept the gifts that the universe wishes to bestow upon you.

In other words, how and when are not your responsibility, but they belong to the universe. This is where divine timing comes in and you must trust that the universe will deliver you the best it has to offer.

Remember to be grateful and Universe will deliver what you desire.

You are now ready to manifest your intentions. Before saying goodbye I have one last gift for you, the next chapter contains a practical example of a manifestation.

PRACTICAL EXAMPLE OF A MANIFESTATION STEP
1: IDENTIFY WHAT YOU WANT TO MANIFEST

You can help yourself in defining what you want to manifest by using the questions I have included in Chapter 7.

- What are my needs?
- What are my wishes?
- Do my needs and desires coincide?

After identifying what you want to manifest (in my example I will make a manifestation to attract more money) use these tips to manifest in the best way you can.

- **I want more money**

Trick 1: The simpler the better. In case of long requests, you can simplify your request into as few words as possible.

In our case you can break down the statement "I want more money" using the actual amount you want.

• **I want more money = I want $100.**

Trick 2: In this case, the statement of the event was simplified by identifying what I want

to attract i.e. one hundred dollars.

This new statement can also be further simplified in its most fundamental elements. When writing numbers, it is better to actually write them down.

• **I want more money. = I want $100. = I want $100.**

I want a hundred dollars is your 'Manifestation'.

Step 2: Manifest your intention in your diary.

Before you start, remember that you have to be present and constant in the routine of the event, constancy is essential to succeed in attracting what you want.

Date: yyyy-mm-dd

- Morning: write your manifestation 3 times in a row. (In our example the manifestation is: One hundred dollars).

1. One hundred dollars
2. One hundred dollars
3. One hundred dollars

- Afternoon: Write your intention 6 times in a row. (In our example the intention is: I receive one hundred dollars).

1. I receive one hundred dollars. (Remember the intention must be made in the present tense)

2. I receive one hundred dollars. (Remember the intention must be made in the present tense)
3. I receive one hundred dollars. (Remember the intention must be made in the present tense)
4. I receive one hundred dollars. (Remember the intention must be made in the present tense)
5. I receive one hundred dollars. (Remember the intention must be made in the present tense)
6. I receive one hundred dollars. (Remember the intention must be made in the present tense)

- Evening: Write your gratitude 9 times in a row.

1. I have a hundred dollars! Thank you, Universe!
2. I have a hundred dollars! Thank you, Universe!
3. I have a hundred dollars! Thank you, Universe!
4. I have a hundred dollars! Thank you, Universe!
5. I have a hundred dollars! Thank you, Universe!
6. I have a hundred dollars! Thank you, Universe!
7. I have a hundred dollars! Thank you, Universe!
8. I have a hundred dollars! Thank you, Universe!
9. I have a hundred dollars! Thank you, Universe!

I am worthy
of success

Write 9 Positive Affirmations

1. ....
2. ....
3. ....
4. ....
5. ....
6. ....
7. ....
8. ....
9. ....

DATE:

3 Morning Manifestations

1. ....
2. ....
3. ....

6 Afternoon Intention

1. ....
2. ....
3. ....
4. ....
5. ....
6. ....

9 Night Gratitude

1. ....
2. ....
3. ....
4. ....
5. ....
6. ....
7. ....
8. ....
9. ....

DATE:

3 Morning Manifestations

1. ....
2. ....
3. ....

6 Afternoon Intention

1. ....
2. ....
3. ....
4. ....
5. ....
6. ....

9 Night Gratitude

1. ....
2. ....
3. ....
4. ....
5. ....
6. ....
7. ....
8. ....
9. ....

MANIFESTATIONS

DATE:

3 Morning Manifestations

1. ....
2. ....
3. ....

6 Afternoon Intention

1. ....
2. ....
3. ....
4. ....
5. ....
6. ....

9 Night Gratitude

1. ....
2. ....
3. ....
4. ....
5. ....
6. ....
7. ....
8. ....
9. ....

DATE:

3 Morning Manifestations

    1. ....
    2. ....
    3. ....

6 Afternoon Intention

    1. ....
    2. ....
    3. ....
    4. ....
    5. ....
    6. ....

9 Night Gratitude

    1. ....
    2. ....
    3. ....
    4. ....
    5. ....
    6. ....
    7. ....
    8. ....
    9. ....

MANIFESTATIONS

DATE:

3 Morning Manifestations

1. ....
2. ....
3. ....

6 Afternoon Intention

1. ....
2. ....
3. ....
4. ....
5. ....
6. ....

9 Night Gratitude

1. ....
2. ....
3. ....
4. ....
5. ....
6. ....
7. ....
8. ....
9. ....

DATE:

3 Morning Manifestations

1. ....
2. ....
3. ....

6 Afternoon Intention

1. ....
2. ....
3. ....
4. ....
5. ....
6. ....

9 Night Gratitude

1. ....
2. ....
3. ....
4. ....
5. ....
6. ....
7. ....
8. ....
9. ....

MANIFESTATIONS

DATE:

3 Morning Manifestations

1. ....
2. ....
3. ....

6 Afternoon Intention

1. ....
2. ....
3. ....
4. ....
5. ....
6. ....

9 Night Gratitude

1. ....
2. ....
3. ....
4. ....
5. ....
6. ....
7. ....
8. ....
9. ....

DATE:

3 Morning Manifestations

1. ....
2. ....
3. ....

6 Afternoon Intention

1. ....
2. ....
3. ....
4. ....
5. ....
6. ....

9 Night Gratitude

1. ....
2. ....
3. ....
4. ....
5. ....
6. ....
7. ....
8. ....
9. ....

DATE:

3 Morning Manifestations

1. ....
2. ....
3. ....

6 Afternoon Intention

1. ....
2. ....
3. ....
4. ....
5. ....
6. ....

9 Night Gratitude

1. ....
2. ....
3. ....
4. ....
5. ....
6. ....
7. ....
8. ....
9. ....

DATE:

3 Morning Manifestations

    1. ....
    2. ....
    3. ....

6 Afternoon Intention

    1. ....
    2. ....
    3. ....
    4. ....
    5. ....
    6. ....

9 Night Gratitude

    1. ....
    2. ....
    3. ....
    4. ....
    5. ....
    6. ....
    7. ....
    8. ....
    9. ....

MANIFESTATIONS

DATE:

3 Morning Manifestations

    1. ....
    2. ....
    3. ....

6 Afternoon Intention

    1. ....
    2. ....
    3. ....
    4. ....
    5. ....
    6. ....

9 Night Gratitude

    1. ....
    2. ....
    3. ....
    4. ....
    5. ....
    6. ....
    7. ....
    8. ....
    9. ....

DATE:

3 Morning Manifestations

1. ....
2. ....
3. ....

6 Afternoon Intention

1. ....
2. ....
3. ....
4. ....
5. ....
6. ....

9 Night Gratitude

1. ....
2. ....
3. ....
4. ....
5. ....
6. ....
7. ....
8. ....
9. ....

DATE:

3 Morning Manifestations

1. ....
2. ....
3. ....

6 Afternoon Intention

1. ....
2. ....
3. ....
4. ....
5. ....
6. ....

9 Night Gratitude

1. ....
2. ....
3. ....
4. ....
5. ....
6. ....
7. ....
8. ....
9. ....

DATE:

3 Morning Manifestations

1. ....
2. ....
3. ....

6 Afternoon Intention

1. ....
2. ....
3. ....
4. ....
5. ....
6. ....

9 Night Gratitude

1. ....
2. ....
3. ....
4. ....
5. ....
6. ....
7. ....
8. ....
9. ....

DATE:

3 Morning Manifestations

   1. ....
   2. ....
   3. ....

6 Afternoon Intention

   1. ....
   2. ....
   3. ....
   4. ....
   5. ....
   6. ....

9 Night Gratitude

   1. ....
   2. ....
   3. ....
   4. ....
   5. ....
   6. ....
   7. ....
   8. ....
   9. ....

DATE:

3 Morning Manifestations

1. ....
2. ....
3. ....

6 Afternoon Intention

1. ....
2. ....
3. ....
4. ....
5. ....
6. ....

9 Night Gratitude

1. ....
2. ....
3. ....
4. ....
5. ....
6. ....
7. ....
8. ....
9. ....

DATE:

3 Morning Manifestations

    1. ....
    2. ....
    3. ....

6 Afternoon Intention

    1. ....
    2. ....
    3. ....
    4. ....
    5. ....
    6. ....

9 Night Gratitude

    1. ....
    2. ....
    3. ....
    4. ....
    5. ....
    6. ....
    7. ....
    8. ....
    9. ....

DATE:

3 Morning Manifestations

1. ....
2. ....
3. ....

6 Afternoon Intention

1. ....
2. ....
3. ....
4. ....
5. ....
6. ....

9 Night Gratitude

1. ....
2. ....
3. ....
4. ....
5. ....
6. ....
7. ....
8. ....
9. ....

MANIFESTATIONS

DATE:

3 Morning Manifestations

1. ....
2. ....
3. ....

6 Afternoon Intention

1. ....
2. ....
3. ....
4. ....
5. ....
6. ....

9 Night Gratitude

1. ....
2. ....
3. ....
4. ....
5. ....
6. ....
7. ....
8. ....
9. ....

DATE:

3 Morning Manifestations

1. ....
2. ....
3. ....

6 Afternoon Intention

1. ....
2. ....
3. ....
4. ....
5. ....
6. ....

9 Night Gratitude

1. ....
2. ....
3. ....
4. ....
5. ....
6. ....
7. ....
8. ....
9. ....

MANIFESTATIONS

DATE:

3 Morning Manifestations

1. ....
2. ....
3. ....

6 Afternoon Intention

1. ....
2. ....
3. ....
4. ....
5. ....
6. ....

9 Night Gratitude

1. ....
2. ....
3. ....
4. ....
5. ....
6. ....
7. ....
8. ....
9. ....

DATE:

3 Morning Manifestations

1. ....
2. ....
3. ....

6 Afternoon Intention

1. ....
2. ....
3. ....
4. ....
5. ....
6. ....

9 Night Gratitude

1. ....
2. ....
3. ....
4. ....
5. ....
6. ....
7. ....
8. ....
9. ....

MANIFESTATIONS

DATE:

3 Morning Manifestations

1. ....
2. ....
3. ....

6 Afternoon Intention

1. ....
2. ....
3. ....
4. ....
5. ....
6. ....

9 Night Gratitude

1. ....
2. ....
3. ....
4. ....
5. ....
6. ....
7. ....
8. ....
9. ....

DATE:

3 Morning Manifestations

1. ....
2. ....
3. ....

6 Afternoon Intention

1. ....
2. ....
3. ....
4. ....
5. ....
6. ....

9 Night Gratitude

1. ....
2. ....
3. ....
4. ....
5. ....
6. ....
7. ....
8. ....
9. ....

DATE:

3 Morning Manifestations

1. ....
2. ....
3. ....

6 Afternoon Intention

1. ....
2. ....
3. ....
4. ....
5. ....
6. ....

9 Night Gratitude

1. ....
2. ....
3. ....
4. ....
5. ....
6. ....
7. ....
8. ....
9. ....

DATE:

3 Morning Manifestations

1. ....
2. ....
3. ....

6 Afternoon Intention

1. ....
2. ....
3. ....
4. ....
5. ....
6. ....

9 Night Gratitude

1. ....
2. ....
3. ....
4. ....
5. ....
6. ....
7. ....
8. ....
9. ....

MANIFESTATIONS

DATE:

3 Morning Manifestations

1. ....
2. ....
3. ....

6 Afternoon Intention

1. ....
2. ....
3. ....
4. ....
5. ....
6. ....

9 Night Gratitude

1. ....
2. ....
3. ....
4. ....
5. ....
6. ....
7. ....
8. ....
9. ....

DATE:

3 Morning Manifestations

1. ....
2. ....
3. ....

6 Afternoon Intention

1. ....
2. ....
3. ....
4. ....
5. ....
6. ....

9 Night Gratitude

1. ....
2. ....
3. ....
4. ....
5. ....
6. ....
7. ....
8. ....
9. ....

MANIFESTATIONS

DATE:

3 Morning Manifestations

    1. ....
    2. ....
    3. ....

6 Afternoon Intention

    1. ....
    2. ....
    3. ....
    4. ....
    5. ....
    6. ....

9 Night Gratitude

    1. ....
    2. ....
    3. ....
    4. ....
    5. ....
    6. ....
    7. ....
    8. ....
    9. ....

DATE:

3 Morning Manifestations

1. ....
2. ....
3. ....

6 Afternoon Intention

1. ....
2. ....
3. ....
4. ....
5. ....
6. ....

9 Night Gratitude

1. ....
2. ....
3. ....
4. ....
5. ....
6. ....
7. ....
8. ....
9. ....

MANIFESTATIONS

DATE:

3 Morning Manifestations

1. ....
2. ....
3. ....

6 Afternoon Intention

1. ....
2. ....
3. ....
4. ....
5. ....
6. ....

9 Night Gratitude

1. ....
2. ....
3. ....
4. ....
5. ....
6. ....
7. ....
8. ....
9. ....

DATE:

3 Morning Manifestations

1. ....
2. ....
3. ....

6 Afternoon Intention

1. ....
2. ....
3. ....
4. ....
5. ....
6. ....

9 Night Gratitude

1. ....
2. ....
3. ....
4. ....
5. ....
6. ....
7. ....
8. ....
9. ....

DATE:

3 Morning Manifestations

1. ....
2. ....
3. ....

6 Afternoon Intention

1. ....
2. ....
3. ....
4. ....
5. ....
6. ....

9 Night Gratitude

1. ....
2. ....
3. ....
4. ....
5. ....
6. ....
7. ....
8. ....
9. ....

DATE:

3 Morning Manifestations

1. ....
2. ....
3. ....

6 Afternoon Intention

1. ....
2. ....
3. ....
4. ....
5. ....
6. ....

9 Night Gratitude

1. ....
2. ....
3. ....
4. ....
5. ....
6. ....
7. ....
8. ....
9. ....

MANIFESTATIONS

DATE:

3 Morning Manifestations

1. ....
2. ....
3. ....

6 Afternoon Intention

1. ....
2. ....
3. ....
4. ....
5. ....
6. ....

9 Night Gratitude

1. ....
2. ....
3. ....
4. ....
5. ....
6. ....
7. ....
8. ....
9. ....

DATE:

3 Morning Manifestations

   1. ....
   2. ....
   3. ....

6 Afternoon Intention

   1. ....
   2. ....
   3. ....
   4. ....
   5. ....
   6. ....

9 Night Gratitude

   1. ....
   2. ....
   3. ....
   4. ....
   5. ....
   6. ....
   7. ....
   8. ....
   9. ....

DATE:

3 Morning Manifestations

1. ....
2. ....
3. ....

6 Afternoon Intention

1. ....
2. ....
3. ....
4. ....
5. ....
6. ....

9 Night Gratitude

1. ....
2. ....
3. ....
4. ....
5. ....
6. ....
7. ....
8. ....
9. ....

DATE:

3 Morning Manifestations

1. ....
2. ....
3. ....

6 Afternoon Intention

1. ....
2. ....
3. ....
4. ....
5. ....
6. ....

9 Night Gratitude

1. ....
2. ....
3. ....
4. ....
5. ....
6. ....
7. ....
8. ....
9. ....

MANIFESTATIONS

DATE:

3 Morning Manifestations

1. ....
2. ....
3. ....

6 Afternoon Intention

1. ....
2. ....
3. ....
4. ....
5. ....
6. ....

9 Night Gratitude

1. ....
2. ....
3. ....
4. ....
5. ....
6. ....
7. ....
8. ....
9. ....

DATE:

3 Morning Manifestations

1. ....
2. ....
3. ....

6 Afternoon Intention

1. ....
2. ....
3. ....
4. ....
5. ....
6. ....

9 Night Gratitude

1. ....
2. ....
3. ....
4. ....
5. ....
6. ....
7. ....
8. ....
9. ....

MANIFESTATIONS

DATE:

3 Morning Manifestations

1. ....
2. ....
3. ....

6 Afternoon Intention

1. ....
2. ....
3. ....
4. ....
5. ....
6. ....

9 Night Gratitude

1. ....
2. ....
3. ....
4. ....
5. ....
6. ....
7. ....
8. ....
9. ....

DATE:

3 Morning Manifestations

1. ....
2. ....
3. ....

6 Afternoon Intention

1. ....
2. ....
3. ....
4. ....
5. ....
6. ....

9 Night Gratitude

1. ....
2. ....
3. ....
4. ....
5. ....
6. ....
7. ....
8. ....
9. ....

MANIFESTATIONS

DATE:

3 Morning Manifestations

    1. ....
    2. ....
    3. ....

6 Afternoon Intention

    1. ....
    2. ....
    3. ....
    4. ....
    5. ....
    6. ....

9 Night Gratitude

    1. ....
    2. ....
    3. ....
    4. ....
    5. ....
    6. ....
    7. ....
    8. ....
    9. ....

DATE:

3 Morning Manifestations

1. ....
2. ....
3. ....

6 Afternoon Intention

1. ....
2. ....
3. ....
4. ....
5. ....
6. ....

9 Night Gratitude

1. ....
2. ....
3. ....
4. ....
5. ....
6. ....
7. ....
8. ....
9. ....

DATE:

3 Morning Manifestations

   1. ....
   2. ....
   3. ....

6 Afternoon Intention

   1. ....
   2. ....
   3. ....
   4. ....
   5. ....
   6. ....

9 Night Gratitude

   1. ....
   2. ....
   3. ....
   4. ....
   5. ....
   6. ....
   7. ....
   8. ....
   9. ....

DATE:

3 Morning Manifestations

1. ....
2. ....
3. ....

6 Afternoon Intention

1. ....
2. ....
3. ....
4. ....
5. ....
6. ....

9 Night Gratitude

1. ....
2. ....
3. ....
4. ....
5. ....
6. ....
7. ....
8. ....
9. ....

MANIFESTATIONS

DATE:

3 Morning Manifestations

1. ....
2. ....
3. ....

6 Afternoon Intention

1. ....
2. ....
3. ....
4. ....
5. ....
6. ....

9 Night Gratitude

1. ....
2. ....
3. ....
4. ....
5. ....
6. ....
7. ....
8. ....
9. ....

DATE:

3 Morning Manifestations

1. ....
2. ....
3. ....

6 Afternoon Intention

1. ....
2. ....
3. ....
4. ....
5. ....
6. ....

9 Night Gratitude

1. ....
2. ....
3. ....
4. ....
5. ....
6. ....
7. ....
8. ....
9. ....

MANIFESTATIONS

DATE:

3 Morning Manifestations

1. ....
2. ....
3. ....

6 Afternoon Intention

1. ....
2. ....
3. ....
4. ....
5. ....
6. ....

9 Night Gratitude

1. ....
2. ....
3. ....
4. ....
5. ....
6. ....
7. ....
8. ....
9. ....

DATE:

3 Morning Manifestations

1. ....
2. ....
3. ....

6 Afternoon Intention

1. ....
2. ....
3. ....
4. ....
5. ....
6. ....

9 Night Gratitude

1. ....
2. ....
3. ....
4. ....
5. ....
6. ....
7. ....
8. ....
9. ....

DATE:

3 Morning Manifestations

1. ....
2. ....
3. ....

6 Afternoon Intention

1. ....
2. ....
3. ....
4. ....
5. ....
6. ....

9 Night Gratitude

1. ....
2. ....
3. ....
4. ....
5. ....
6. ....
7. ....
8. ....
9. ....

DATE:

3 Morning Manifestations

   1. ....
   2. ....
   3. ....

6 Afternoon Intention

   1. ....
   2. ....
   3. ....
   4. ....
   5. ....
   6. ....

9 Night Gratitude

   1. ....
   2. ....
   3. ....
   4. ....
   5. ....
   6. ....
   7. ....
   8. ....
   9. ....

DATE:

3 Morning Manifestations

1. ....
2. ....
3. ....

6 Afternoon Intention

1. ....
2. ....
3. ....
4. ....
5. ....
6. ....

9 Night Gratitude

1. ....
2. ....
3. ....
4. ....
5. ....
6. ....
7. ....
8. ....
9. ....

DATE:

3 Morning Manifestations

1. ....
2. ....
3. ....

6 Afternoon Intention

1. ....
2. ....
3. ....
4. ....
5. ....
6. ....

9 Night Gratitude

1. ....
2. ....
3. ....
4. ....
5. ....
6. ....
7. ....
8. ....
9. ....

MANIFESTATIONS

DATE:

3 Morning Manifestations

    1. ....
    2. ....
    3. ....

6 Afternoon Intention

    1. ....
    2. ....
    3. ....
    4. ....
    5. ....
    6. ....

9 Night Gratitude

    1. ....
    2. ....
    3. ....
    4. ....
    5. ....
    6. ....
    7. ....
    8. ....
    9. ....

DATE:

3 Morning Manifestations

1. ....
2. ....
3. ....

6 Afternoon Intention

1. ....
2. ....
3. ....
4. ....
5. ....
6. ....

9 Night Gratitude

1. ....
2. ....
3. ....
4. ....
5. ....
6. ....
7. ....
8. ....
9. ....

DATE:

3 Morning Manifestations

1. ....
2. ....
3. ....

6 Afternoon Intention

1. ....
2. ....
3. ....
4. ....
5. ....
6. ....

9 Night Gratitude

1. ....
2. ....
3. ....
4. ....
5. ....
6. ....
7. ....
8. ....
9. ....

DATE:

3 Morning Manifestations

1. ....
2. ....
3. ....

6 Afternoon Intention

1. ....
2. ....
3. ....
4. ....
5. ....
6. ....

9 Night Gratitude

1. ....
2. ....
3. ....
4. ....
5. ....
6. ....
7. ....
8. ....
9. ....

DATE:

3 Morning Manifestations

    1. ....
    2. ....
    3. ....

6 Afternoon Intention

    1. ....
    2. ....
    3. ....
    4. ....
    5. ....
    6. ....

9 Night Gratitude

    1. ....
    2. ....
    3. ....
    4. ....
    5. ....
    6. ....
    7. ....
    8. ....
    9. ....

DATE:

3 Morning Manifestations

1. ....
2. ....
3. ....

6 Afternoon Intention

1. ....
2. ....
3. ....
4. ....
5. ....
6. ....

9 Night Gratitude

1. ....
2. ....
3. ....
4. ....
5. ....
6. ....
7. ....
8. ....
9. ....

MANIFESTATIONS

DATE:

3 Morning Manifestations

1. ....
2. ....
3. ....

6 Afternoon Intention

1. ....
2. ....
3. ....
4. ....
5. ....
6. ....

9 Night Gratitude

1. ....
2. ....
3. ....
4. ....
5. ....
6. ....
7. ....
8. ....
9. ....

DATE:

3 Morning Manifestations

   1. ....
   2. ....
   3. ....

6 Afternoon Intention

   1. ....
   2. ....
   3. ....
   4. ....
   5. ....
   6. ....

9 Night Gratitude

   1. ....
   2. ....
   3. ....
   4. ....
   5. ....
   6. ....
   7. ....
   8. ....
   9. ....

DATE:

3 Morning Manifestations

1. ....
2. ....
3. ....

6 Afternoon Intention

1. ....
2. ....
3. ....
4. ....
5. ....
6. ....

9 Night Gratitude

1. ....
2. ....
3. ....
4. ....
5. ....
6. ....
7. ....
8. ....
9. ....

DATE:

3 Morning Manifestations

1. ....
2. ....
3. ....

6 Afternoon Intention

1. ....
2. ....
3. ....
4. ....
5. ....
6. ....

9 Night Gratitude

1. ....
2. ....
3. ....
4. ....
5. ....
6. ....
7. ....
8. ....
9. ....

MANIFESTATIONS

DATE:

3 Morning Manifestations

1. ....
2. ....
3. ....

6 Afternoon Intention

1. ....
2. ....
3. ....
4. ....
5. ....
6. ....

9 Night Gratitude

1. ....
2. ....
3. ....
4. ....
5. ....
6. ....
7. ....
8. ....
9. ....

DATE:

3 Morning Manifestations

1. ....
2. ....
3. ....

6 Afternoon Intention

1. ....
2. ....
3. ....
4. ....
5. ....
6. ....

9 Night Gratitude

1. ....
2. ....
3. ....
4. ....
5. ....
6. ....
7. ....
8. ....
9. ....

Made in the USA
Middletown, DE
05 October 2023

40322670R00057